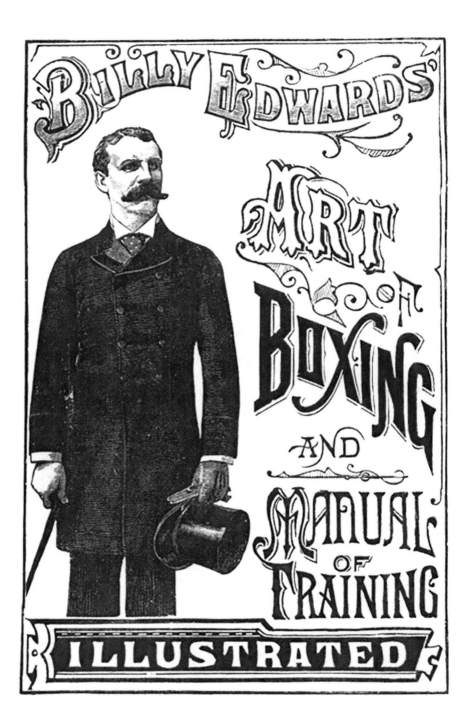

BILLY EDWARDS'

ART OF BOXING AND MANUAL OF TRAINING

ILLUSTRATED

THE ART OF BOXING
AND MANUAL OF TRAINING

THE DELUXE EDITION

WILLIAM "BILLY" EDWARDS

Former Lightweight Champion

Edited
by
JAMES BISHOP

Promethean Press

The Art of Boxing and Manual of Training
Deluxe Edition

Promethean Press
PO Box 5572
Frisco, TX 75035
www.promethean-press.com

ISBN: 978-0-9810202-2-8

Manufactured in the United States of America

TABLE OF CONTENTS

PART FOUR: THE RULES

ADDENDUM

THE ART OF BOXING

AND MANUAL OF TRAINING

INTRODUCTION

William "Make-Believe Billy" Edwards was one of the pioneers of American boxing. From the earliest days of bare-knuckled fighting until the later advent of of rule-based glove matches, Edwards was at the forefront of the art as a fighter, trainer, and scholar.

Born on December 21, 1844 in Birmingham, England, Edwards journeyed to the United States to find his fame and fortune in the American ring. On August 24, 1868, Edwards fought Sam Collyer to earn the title of lightweight champion. He would hold the title for four years, defending it against such boxers as Tim Collins and Arthur Chambers from 1868 to 1872.

William Edwards was known as a quick fighter who hit hard and countered well. Outside the ring, Edwards was considered an amiable man of considerable modesty.

One interesting distinction in William Edwards' career was boxing a future president of the United States. In the late 1870s Edwards appeared for a sparring exhibition at Harvard University. When Edwards asked the students for a volunteer to spar with him, an adventurous Teddy Roosevelt stepped up. A classmate of Roosevelt's would later note that within a couple of minutes "Edwards had banged him until he was ready to acknowledge there was a vast difference between a college amateur and a professional ringster."

William Edwards' last fight was against Charlie Mitchell on May 12, 1884. By that time Edwards was 39 years of age and far past his prime. By the third round, Edwards was so badly beaten that the fight had to be stopped by the police. After the Mitchell fight, Edwards retired.

In 1882, William Edwards became the house detective for the Hoffman House Hotel on Broadway and 25th Street in New York, a position he held until 1896 when he became a full-time boxing

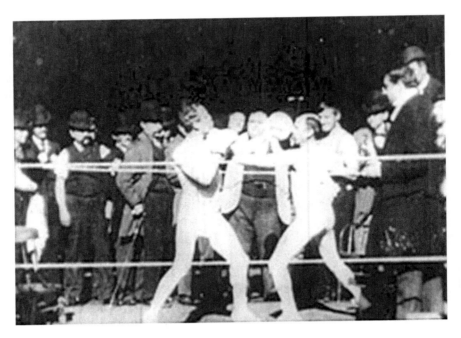

trainer. His students during this time included the legendary John L. Sullivan.

William Edwards has the historical distinction of being one of only a handful of nineteenth century boxers to be captured on film; Black Maria Studios filmed him in 1895 during his participation in a five-round exhibition match. Only one round of the footage is known to exist today.

During the time William Edwards worked for the Hoffman House, he was much sought after as an authority on the art of pugilism. In 1888 he wrote *The Art of Boxing and Manual of Training* with the help of his friend and former opponent, Arthur Chambers. The manual featured boxing techniques as well as tips on diet and exercise. The book also included the various rules governing ringcraft, most notably the American Fair-Play Rules. Their inclusion would result in the book being used as a reference in a landmark 1895 Supreme Court case which pitted the state of Louisiana against boxing in New Orleans.

In later years, William Edwards became a successful real estate investor and family man. Edwards died on August 12, 1907, at the age of 63. He is remembered today as one of the pre-eminent boxers of the 19th century and a member of the International Boxing Hall of Fame.

James Bishop

PREFACE

My reasons for venturing before the public with a work on the art of boxing and science of self-defense are few and simple, but I trust, when understood, will be considered just and appropriate. In the first place, then, be it said that although it is an admitted fact that the good old palmy days of the prize ring have passed away, and lusty manhood is no longer allowed, by law, to exhibit to his fellow man, in their most perfect and scientifically developed character, those grand attributes of physical power, strength, nerve, pluck, endurance, determination, and courage, that we all profess to admire, and the lack of which we resent as a stigma unworthy to be borne, still, I am glad to say that there yet remains a very large majority of right-minded people who approve and support the art of boxing as a wholesome and legitimate means of physical recreation and exercise, enjoyed for the purpose of benefiting our bodily health and condition. And although for the past twenty years I have been engaged either in the active, public pursuit of my profession, or at least in close and intimate relations with those who were and are its leading lights and exponents, I have never yet found a thoroughly reliable and useful text-book that could, in any way, assist the pupil to practice and perform the lessons with the gloves given by the professor. Such a book I modestly ventured to think I could more or less successfully produce, and the attempt I here submit with the assurance that, in its preparation, I have been guided by the wish of doing my profession a service, and of showing that, if properly and judiciously practiced, boxing is entitled to the social recognition its many sterling merits command.

In order that the pupil may readily and clearly grasp the different evolutions, blows, and guards the text explains, accurate illustrations are imperative, and in all former manuals on the subject this was the most serious and detrimental fault. Instantaneous photography has, however, made the swiftest movements capable of reproduction, and so I secured the hearty cooperation and assistance of my old friend and fellow-pugilist, Arthur Chambers, of Philadelphia, ex-Champion Lightweight of America and England, than whom there are few cleverer boxers, and, together, we had a regular friendly "set-to" with the gloves, and by the aid of an expert photographer every evolution of the context was caught, as either one or the other of us put it into practice, and the result, so every authority unhesitatingly states, is the best set of boxing pictures ever yet placed on the market.

In order that my friends, patrons, and the public may be satisfied that I am competent to speak authoritatively on the noble art I have practiced and taught for years, I have thought it might interest them to read a short biography of my principal prize-ring battles and glove fights, and also the career of Arthur Chambers. I therefore append these notices, and beg to remain,

Respectfully,

WILLIAM EDWARDS
Hoffman House
Madison Square
New York City

PART ONE
HISTORICAL

A SHORT SKETCH OF BILLY EDWARDS

William Edwards, for many years the champion lightweight of America, was born at Birmingham, Warwickshire, England, on the 21st of December, 1844. When he was nine years of age he back to knock about that grimy town as an errand-boy, with light curly hair and soft blue eyes, lithe and active as a kitten, and always passionately fond of boxing and sparring. He was early put to work at the foundry, and soon was rolling railway pins. He took readily to all manner of outdoor sports, and was renowned among his fellows for running, jumping, and wrestling. His parents, while Edwards was yet a lad, removed to Staffordshire. The "black" country, as the inhabitants call that region of coal-fields and factories, has always been celebrated for its fighting population, and Billy had his hands full all the time fighting boys who asserted their right to be considered "cock of the walk" in the neighborhood. He fought his first battle for money when he was sixteen at Smethwick, Staffordshire, and won his maiden victory against the local featherweight champion on a sharp and bloody fight lasting 30 minutes.

Edwards next removed to London and worked at iron ship-building. He was employed in one of the great shipbuilding establishments on the Isle of Dogs in the East End of London, opposite of Greenwich. He was employed in the construction of the ram Valiant, and afterwards on the British man-o'-war *Northumberland*. The Isle of Dogs was as noted for its local prizefighters as the "black" country, and Edwards had many an off-hand encounter in which he was generally victor - his most stubborn opponent being the bully of the yard in which he worked named "Castiron" Collins, whom he had badly beaten when the authorities interfered.

In May, 1865, at the age of one and twenty, Edwards came to America in search of employment at his trade. He found work in

New York City and started at boiler making. While on the docs at 11th St., E. R., Billy fell foul of the most noted pugilist of those parts, a man weighing upwards of 170 pounds, but our hero went for him though he only scaled 145 pounds, and in a very severe battle, lasting 45 minutes, he whipped him completely.

His evenings were spent in visiting the principal sporting houses and boxing resorts in the city, where he sparred at benefits and exhibitions. At the Assembly Rooms, corner of Elizabeth and Grand Sts., he sparred at Jack Turner's benefit in the fall of 1865. He also had set-tos with Sol Aaron, brother of the celebrated Barney Aaron, and with Mike Coburn, brother of the champion, Jo Coburn. He also appeared at the benefits of Jim Elliot and Bill Davis. In these exhibitions young Edwards displayed such remarkable prowess and ability, so much pluck, dexterity and quickness in the handling of the "mittens," that he was eagerly sought after by men who wanted to learn the art of boxing, and he soon gained so many pupils that he concluded to give up his trade, and joined the famous Van Slyke, one of the cleverest boxers of that day, and who, for the past thirty years, has been teaching, and may still be heard from at his well-known place of business, above Daly's Theatre, Broadway.

In 1866 he posted $1,000 to fight Jim Fox, the lightweight pugilist, but could not come to terms, and articles were never signed. In '67 Edwards issued an all world challenge to fight any man at 128 pounds for $1,000 a side and the lightweight championship but nothing came of it.

"Billy" was by this time well and favorably known to the leading lights of the fraternity, and by his modest, unassuming manners, his frank and genial disposition, had made a large number of friends. His reputation as a quick and scientific boxer was widespread, and his friends were eager to see him try his metal on a "foeman worthy of his steel." They did not have long to seek an antagonist. Sam Collyer was at that time the champion lightweight of America, and had proved his claim to the title in six hard-fought fields. Billy was too good a man to waste his time on second-rate competitors, and was willing to cast his dye for fame on the chance of a battle with the best in the land. He was now finely developed and in the prime of vigor, age, and condition. He stood 5 feet 4 5/8 inches in his stockings, with a clear complexion, though somewhat pale. He was splendidly built, with wonderful muscular development of the arms, chest, and shoulders. His loins and lower extremities were somewhat slim, but he made up for this defect by wonderful agility in getting round.

His maiden effort in a twenty-four-foot prize ring was on the 24th of August, 1868, when at Travers' Island, Ship Neck, Cove River, Va., he met Sam Collyer for $1,000 a side and the lightweight championship of America. He was seconded by Dooney Harris and Barney Aaron, and weighed 124 pounds as he entered the ring. The day was swelteringly hot, and both men found training at that time of year a most severe ordeal. The fight at first seemed to go rather against our hero, but he had not earned the title of "the gamest man in the ring" for nothing, and he stuck to his man with indomitable pluck and perseverance. The fight was stubbornly contested, round by round, but during the latter part of the battle Sam Collyer seemed to lose heart and strength, while Billy seemed to grow stronger and fresher the longer he stayed in the ring. Eventually, after one hour and 14 minutes, in which 47 fierce rounds had been fought, Edwards knocked his man out, and was hailed victor and champion.

After his victory over Collyer, he took a tour through the country with Dooney Harris, giving a series of boxing entertainments in all the principal cities of the Union. In 1869 Billy went for a three-months' trip to England, and he visited most of the principal cities of his native kingdom, giving sparring entertainments, and meeting the best men of the day at the different towns he visited. On returning from England, Edwards went into partnership with famous Harry Hill, and together they ran their famous place in Centre Street. While there Billy got on his second match with Sam Collyer, who was still smarting from his signal defeat in 1868. They met at Mystic Island on the 2nd of March, 1870, and the stakes were, as before, $1,000 and the championship. They both fought at 124 pounds and in 47 minutes Edwards gave Collyer his *coup de grace*, knocking him insensible, and he did not recover from the effect of the blow for upwards of three hours.

On May 25th, 1871, Billy met Tim Collins, a protégé of the well-known Nat Langham, at Cypress Hills, Long Island, for the lightweight championship and $1,000 a side. The battle was hotly contested, and when darkness closed in upon the scene neither had

had enough. Ninety-five rounds were fought, and both men received severe punishment.

After this fight, Billy joined the Brothers Jim and Pooley Mace, and traveled as far as California, giving boxing exhibitions, and meeting all comers. In Chicago he had a set-to with Professor Laflin; at Sacramento he met Scotty, of Brooklyn. In San Francisco he encountered Tommy Chandler, Barney Farley, and Denny Haley; also White, of Australia. He sparred with Jim Mace at Council Bluffs.

In 1872 a challenge was issued by "The Unknown" to fight anybody at 124 pounds, for $1,000 and the championship. The dark horse turned out to be the famous Bat Mullins of London, a quondam associate of Arthur Chambers in Shaw's boxing-place in Windmill Street, London; but the match was not taken on with Mullins, and Arthur Chambers was substituted in his place. This famous battle, which is still looked back to as the grandest fight since Tom Sayers and Heenan had their memorable set-to, came off at Walpole Island, Mount Clair River, Canada. It was for $2,000 a side and the championship. The struggle lasted one hour and 35 minutes, when William Tracy, the referee, gave the victory to Arthur on the supposition that Edwards fouled him in the 35th round by biting him in the back. After events proved that the whole fight was a put-up job on the part of Jim Mace and Barney Aaron, Edward's seconds, in collusion with the referee, Tracy, to give the fight to Chambers. It was afterwards proved that Chambers was bitten by his own second, Seddons. Be that as it may, there was undoubtedly much unfair play, though neither man at the break-up was badly punished. From the *Herald* account, which I have before me as I write, it seems that Edwards was getting the best of it, and if it had been fought to a finish would probably have won.

After the Chambers fight, Billy again was seen sparring at benefits and the like, keeping constantly before the sporting fraternity, and winning golden opinions from everybody by his straightforward, manly bearing, his affable manners, and his genial, amiable disposition. In the next year he visited England again, and met William Fawcett, a very clever boxer of Birmingham. He was again victorious, after a tremendous struggle of 100 rounds.

His old antagonist, Sam Collyer, was at him again, for the third time, on his return from England, and Billy accommodated him, on the same old terms, on the 13th of August, 1874. Both men entered the ring at catch-weights - Billy being the lighter by about 10 pounds. This, however, did not make any difference, as he did his man up in ten rounds in 22 minutes. This was our champion's last appearance in the magic ring, and he retired from the prize ring with the proud record of never having been vanquished in a battle. Billy is to be found any evening at the Hoffman House, where his quiet and modest behavior has earned him a host of friends, and it may safely be said that there never was a more popular man in the profession than the famous lightweight champion of America, Billy Edwards.

These short biographies of the two boxers who appear in the cuts that illustrate Edwards' book on the art of boxing ought to satisfy anybody that he is a competent authority to preach and to teach what he so very ably practiced.

A SHORT SKETCH OF ARTHUR CHAMBERS

Arthur Chambers, the subject of this short sketch, was born on the 3rd of December, 1847, in the little town of Salford, which is situated across the river from Manchester, Lancashire, England. He served for some years in the Royal Navy, and for eighteen months was the gun-room boy of the British man-of-war *St. George*, and during the years 1862-63 had the distinguished honor of looking after His Royal Highness Prince Alfred, Duke of Edinburgh, and with him he cruised with the Channel Squadron all through the Mediterranean Sea.

The free and healthy regular life of a man-o'-war did much to build up and develop an unusually strong and muscular constitution, and the active duties of the ship's boy taught him that agility and nimbleness on his feet for which he was after wards so preeminently remarkable in the prize ring. Young chambers had ample opportunities while afloat to become initiated into the mysteries of the fistic art, for it is even still a good old custom in the navy, during fair and pleasant weather, to allow the blue-jackets to skylark during the second dog-watch, which is between four and six o'clock in the evening, and on such occasions the gloves were always a very favorite amusement. In these friendly encounters our embryo champion took an active and constant part, and early displayed such quickness of movement and such an aptitude to learn every new wrinkle, that he soon became known as the smartest featherweight boxer in the ship, and at the age of 16 was the "cock" of the boys, and could easily whip any one of his own weight in the fleet. These early successes evidently turned his thoughts toward the prize ring, and made him decide that in profession he would be able to turn to the best account the sturdy talents of which he was possessed. In order to get clear of the navy he feigned sickness, and while on duty one day, dropped suddenly on the deck in violent spasms and convulsions, foaming and frothing at the mouth by the friendly aid of a piece of soap, which he slipped into his mouth to produce this effect, and which melted and had to be swallowed before medical aid led to its discovery. He was invalided from the service as being subject to fits of epilepsy and returned to his native town of Salford. Here he continued his pugilistic training and education, and on the 1st of October, 1864, he "faced his man." His opponent was Arthur Webber, a local lightweight celebrity, whom he easily vanquished in a short and sharp set-to of 20 rounds in 35 minutes. He was now 19 years of age, stiffly and compactly built, standing in his stocking feet 5 feet 33/4 inches, but Bell's Life, of London, has always quoted him at 5 feet 4 and 1/2 inches, accrediting him with three-quarters of an inch that does belong to him. When in fighting trim he tipped the scales at about 116 to 118 pounds, with a chest measurement of 40 inches. He has a very high, florid complexion; frank, bright blue eyes, and his natural temperament is light-hearted, genial, and good-natured.

His second appearance in the prize ring was against Ned Evans, of Ardwick, much his superior at that time in pugilistic accomplishments, but he was no match for Arthur in physical endurance, and he secured another victory. After vanquishing Ned Allen, Chambers and he became intimate, and when on February 6, 1899, he met James Prior for two hundred and fifty dollars a side, Ned Allen "looked after" Chambers. The fight was short, sharp, and decisive, for in 13 rounds, lasting only 20 minutes, Arthur had his man whipped. *Bell's Life*, speaking of him in connection with this fight, says: "He is a lad with excellent shoulders and loins, exceedingly strong and game, with tremendous punishing powers, but capable of taking any amount of punishment himself." In fact Arthur at this time was considered one of the strongest men of his weight in the country, and deserved the summing up of his qualities as given by the same sporting journal before quoted, when it said, "he was a compact bundle of muscular Christianity."

The next fight was with James Brady for two hundred and fifty dollars a side, and the lightweight championship of the "Midland Circuit." He was trained by Ned Allen at Ardwick, and entered the ring in the very pink of condition at 116 pounds. This was in many respects a most remarkable fight, as well in the exciting incidents of the affair, as the indomitable pluck an obstinacy displayed by both men. The first day they fought for one hour and 20 minutes until interfered by the authorities, and on the next day they made up the time to three hours, 15 minutes, fighting in all 63 rounds, until Chambers was hit completely blind but still had an excellent and serviceable pair of hands, and was sound and strong on his feet. His antagonist, on the other hand, was almost powerless from exhaustion, being very "groggy" on his pins, while his fists were swollen to the size of his head; but he could just see daylight from one of his peepers and so the fight went against Chambers. *Bell's Life* concluded its remarks thus: "As may be naturally anticipated, both men were most severely punished, and the loser shed tears of mortifications at the result. A gamer or more determined battle was never witnessed, and Chambers deserves to be remembered by his backers for the tenacity and bravery he displayed to achieve the victory."

On February 19, 1867, Arthur found himself face to face with Bob Goodwin, and an obstinate fight was the result. Goodwin pursued the same tactics as were resorted to by Jem Smith in his recent fight with Jake Kilrain, and went down repeatedly to avoid punishment. The battle lasted two hours and 20 minutes, 105 rounds being fought. It was a dead sure thing for Chambers when the police robbed him of a well-earned victory. Jim Finch was his next victim, at Aldershott, on May 18th the same year. He won his sixth triumph in one hour and 40 minutes, fighting 62 rounds.

He was now well and favorably known to the lovers of the prize ring throughout the country, and was intimate with all the leading pugilists of that day. He knew Jim Mace, Joe Gross, Tom King, and all the other worthies. During the years of 1867 and '68, Arthur, with Bat Mullins, another well-known lightweight, conducted the boxing and lessons at Billy Shaw's famous resort in Windmill St., Haymarket, London. He now was admittedly the best lightweight in the country, and found some difficulty in being accommodated with a customer. He endeavored to get on a match with Jim Lead, Alec Lawson, and his old antagonist Jim Brady, but without avail. In December, 1868, he issued an all-round challenge to fight any one at 8 stone 4 lbs., but could not get a match on. In 1868, he went back to his own town of Salford, and started a sporting resort of his own, known as "The Sportsman's Inn." Later he fought and whipped Harry Kimberly in 33 rounds, in one hour and 23 minutes, though the fight was broken up by roughs; and also defeated Tom Scattergood in a match at eight stone two libs. As champion light-weight of the world, he arrived in America in 1871, and held that distinction till he retired from the ring the day he fought Tom Clark. He has been prominently identified with the leading events of the ring in this country, and is still to be heard from at his present head-quarters, "Champion's Rest," Ridge Avenue, Philadelphia. Arthur Chambers, of late years has been industrious in promoting and fostering the interesting sport of dog racing, and the sweepstakes held at Olympic Park, in Philadelphia, are now widely and favor-ably known. He was the first man to introduce this exciting sport into this country, and now owns one of the finest kennels of the strain of dogs used. He has also been the friend and encourager of pedestrianism; and in Philadelphia, on Thanksgiving Day last year, he distributed five hundred dollars in prizes among profes-sional runners, and one hundred dollars in prizes for the dog hand-icaps. Arthur has gained hosts of friends by the honest and liberal way he has conducted his business; he has never in any way been connected with any crooked transactions, either in the prize ring or on the cinderpath, and is looked upon as one of the best trainers and teachers America has ever had. May he long continue to fol-low the same creditable course.

Nothing has been said in this history of his famous battle with his friend, Billy Edwards, for an account of which the reader is referred to the sketch of that famous boxer's public life.

PART TWO
TRAINING AND PREPARATION

A INTRODUCTORY REMARKS

It seems almost a pity that such a noble and manly exercise as that of boxing, should, from want of proper support, be still fast falling into oblivion and disrepute. When practiced by gentlemen as a means of muscular development, there is not an exercise that gives such grand and lasting results. Look at a man that is a master of the science, and mark the free and graceful movement of every limb. There is nothing stiff, ungainly or loutish about the boxer. His head is carried erect and firm, supported by a full, strong neck, in which the muscles stand out clear and well defined. His eye is bright and flashing, but with a quiet, observant watchfulness that plainly indicates that nothing escapes it. When his gaze meets yours he looks you squarely and firmly in the eyes; there is no uneasy shifting and glancing from side to side. His shoulders are broad, but graceful and sloping, and from the arms, with full and rounded biceps, fall so easily and naturally to their proper position at the sides. The elbows follow the beautiful curves of the body, and are not stuck out from the ribs and flapped like the helpless flutterings of a half-fledged gosling in its futile efforts to fly, which is the general way one sees the arms carried by would be swells on our fashionable thoroughfares. The chest expansive, and well filled out, shows plenty of room for the lungs to work. The deltoid and shoulder muscles are all thoroughly developed, and go to form a strong and shapely back. The whole trunk presents a rounded, symmetrical, and perfect appearance that is pleasant to look at, and makes one feel instinctively what a grand and wonderful piece of mechanism man really is, when all his inherent qualities of strength have been made the most of.

How free and elastic, too, his step! The full and shapely thighs work clean and straight form the hip, impress one with a sense of stability and power. His progress is resolute, even and steady; no shambling, slovenly gait can be part of a man who depends as much on the nimbleness and agility with which he gets about on his legs to keep him out of reach of his antagonist, as he does on the dexterity of his hands and the keenness of his sight. And then, too, how firm, smooth, and clear is the skin of the boxer. The constant exercise, by inducing vigorous perspiration, the many rubbings with the towel and hand, open and keep free from impurities every pore of the skin, and render them ever ready to perform their allotted functions. And let me point out, in this connection, what important benefits to our system result from those exercises that induce free and wholesome perspiration. By getting rid of much of the accumulated secretions of the body, it aids and strengthens two very important organs of our physical economy-the liver and the kidneys-whose function it is to keep eliminating from the system those impurities that are daily absorbed by the pores of the skin, as also those that are taken up internally. And were it not that these organs were assisted in their duties by the cleansing process that takes place every time one perspires, they would find their task more than they could thoroughly perform, and would either get prematurely worn out, or become diseased by overwork and abnormal activity, and the body would, in consequence, become impaired in health. In fact, it is a recognized fact that many of the ailments that have their origin in the unhealthy condition of these organs can be readily traced to those sedentary and lazy habits that shirk sufficient exercise to produce perspiration; and one of the surest remedies resorted to in relieving disease of the lungs or kidneys, is to cause the patient, either by exercise or by artificial means, to perspire profusely at regular intervals.

Besides these and many other incalculable benefits to the body which can be acquired as effectively by no such other means as by boxing, the practice of the art of self-defense lays up a stock of mental good qualities in the boxer that endear him and make him admired and esteemed by his fellow men. Knowing that he can, at extremity, protect himself from ill treatment, he is more tolerant and patient in his intercourse with others. Boxing also makes a man self-reliant and resourceful when assailed by sudden or unexpected dangers or difficulties. The same courage and determination that makes him face a personal antagonist, is of immense value to him in overcoming the stern obstacles of daily life. The pluck and

powers of endurance and recuperation gained in friendly bouts with the gloves, are brought into much finer effect when opposed to the real buffets and blows of ill-fortune and adversity. The command of temper essential to success in boxing (for if you lose your head, skill with your hands will serve you little against an opponent master of both) makes a man competent to command in delicate situations, where tact and temper are more avail than brute force.

And even if the many excellent results directly traceable to this healthy exercise were not sufficient to popularize it, one would suppose the natural law of self-protection incentive enough to induce the majority to learn something of boxing.

To every animal a kind Providence has bestowed more or less adequate weapons of offense and defense, and it is a singular fact that man, the noblest creature, is the worst off in this respect, and in the use of bare means supplied by nature, is the least expert of them all. Without the assistance of those weapons that his ingenuity has invented, his hands are unfit to stand an encounter with an enemy much his inferior in size and strength. But, on the other hand, skill in the proper and dexterous use of the hands, coupled with the agility of movement learnt in boxing school, has often been the means of enabling man to subdue and gain the mastery over animals many times his superior in strength.

Let me instance a case in point: A very vicious and ill-tempered horse was eating his head off in a luxuriant loose box, because there was no one in the establishment of the gentleman to whom he belonged who had the courage or strength to enter his stable and saddle and bridle him. If a groom approached for any other purpose than to give him his corn and hay, he would speedily drive him a way by a free use of his hoofs and teeth. One day at lunch his owner was lamenting the uselessness of the finest horse in his stud, to a party of friends, and wound up by saying that he would gladly make the horse a present to any one who could saddle and rid him out of the yard. A young graduate of Oxford expressed his willingness to make the attempt, and though warned by many a blood-curdling recital of what had been the fate of grooms and stable-boys that had made the like effort, he persisted in his determination to try. After lunch, all adjourned to the stable in the expectation of seeing the young fellow receive a severe lesson for his temerity. He was known to be an expert in every manly exercise, especially boxing, and was in perfect wind and training. Selecting a saddle and bridle from an adjacent rack, he approached the strong bars that opened into the brute's stall, speaking kindly and soothingly to him. The horse turned and eyed the stranger, and catching sight of the hated bit, became furious, lashing out madly with his heels, and stamping wildly about the stall, making the straw of his bedding fly in every direction. Without a word, the graduate rested the saddle and bridle on the top rail; but the steady, undaunted fire of the eye, the firmly compressed lip, the backward poise of the shapely head, the swelling muscles of his lithe and active frame as he lightly vaulted into the box, told plainly of the iron, indomitable will and pluck within. Scarcely had he landed on his feet than the now thoroughly infuriated beast came rushing headlong at him with its satin ears flattened closely against its lean head, its eyes aflame and bloodshot, its mouth agape, and displaying a set of gleaming teeth, which he gnashed and ground with fury. Sudden and savage though the onslaught was, the young Oxonian was prepared. Throwing himself naturally and gracefully into boxing attitude, he met the maddened animal with a blow on the temple, just between the ear and the eye, swift, straight, and inexorable as from a Nasmyth's hammer, that brought him on his knees. Rearing up and squealing with pain and rage, the brute again rushed upon his foe, who had stepped aside, but pale and determined, awaited his coming. Again like a levin bolt, straight from the shoulder, flew the clenched fist, and down dropped the horse. Slowly he staggered to his feet, and trembling in every limb, while great patches of perspiration stained his flanks at sides, he cowered in a corner of the stall, completely vanquished. The victor soon had the bit in his mouth and the saddle on his back, and, leading him out of the stall, cantered gaily away on the prize his bravery and knowledge of boxing had won.

PREPARATORY TRAINING

In order to enjoy to the fullest extent the advantages acquired by a regular use of the gloves, and to be ready at all times to put into practice the useful lessons learnt in boxing, it is necessary that the body be kept in a course of auxiliary exercise and moderately abstemious habits of living; and it will be readily admitted that such a violent exertion as boxing cannot be indulged in without bad effects, unless the body is in a state fit to bear the strain.

A man, therefore, who intends boxing to be to him a pleasant and sterling means of relaxation, will do well to be moderate in all things. Of the many excesses that sap the system, there are none so disastrous as drinking and smoking. By this it is not meant that total abstinence from either is absolutely demanded, but the less of them you can do with, the better for your wind and general condition.

The above advice is meant to refer only to the ordinary training sufficient to keep the general amateur athlete in good condition; but when a professional in undergoing the severe training that will put him into the fittest condition to enter a championship running or rowing match, or undertake a battle in the prize ring, it is imperative that he abstain entirely from the user of tobacco; and he can only take such liquids and stimulants as are authorized by his trainer

Regular hours for meals and for retiring and rising must be practiced. Rise, therefore, betimes, refreshed by a sound night's rest, and do not neglect the invigorating effects of the morning plunge, which washes off the surface of the skin, and the friction of a good rough towel opens all the pores of the body, and puts them in working order to perform their proper functions during the day.

Do not take any violent exercise before breakfast. During the hours of sleep the fires that feed vitality have been "banked" so to speak, and fresh fuel should be added before expecting the machine to run with a full head of steam. The first meal should be hearty, though somewhat lighter than the midday repast, which, to all exercising people, should be *the* meal of the day. A couple of chops or a tender piece of steak are always admissible, or a good plate of cold beef is not amiss. If you can relish it, let your meats always be eaten rather "under done," for, if too much cooked, the blood, which is the life and strength, is apt to become dried out.

Breakfast Diet

Be sparing at all your meals of eating starchy sub-stances, such as potatoes, rice, farina, etc., and take stale in preference to newly-baked bread; or, what is bet-ter still, eat pilot bread, or any other kind of plain, light biscuit. Hot rolls and fancy cakes, or corn bread take a great deal longer to digest, and are not, therefore, con-ducive to good wind. Don't drink a great deal of what in training parlance is termed "slops." A good-sized breakfast cup of not too strong coffee or tea ought to be ample for a healthy man, though the latter beverage is the one that should have the preference. Don't indulge in large draughts of new milk; it is very fattening and too rich, and goes rather to the flesh and fat than to muscle. In England, where many man leading an active, out-of-door life are accustomed to drink beer with their breakfast, a glass of ale may be taken, but this is not to be recommended, and should never be thought of if your are not in the habit of drinking beer at this meal.

Smoking

Don't smoke after breakfast, nor, in fact, at any time during the day. There is nothing so pernicious to the wind as the use of tobacco, and this fact cannot be laid down in too strong terms to those who may wish to put themselves in training, no matter for what exercise; and go stringent is the rule, that professionals, when going into hard training for any special event, be it rowing running, boxing, or swimming, are not allowed to breathe the fumes of tobacco, *even in the open air.*

After breakfast you are ready to begin work in real earnest; and many are the different exercises that offer themselves to your consideration for preparing you generally for the scientific lessons of the afternoon or evening, and all of them are intended to work up and elaborate some particular part of the body.

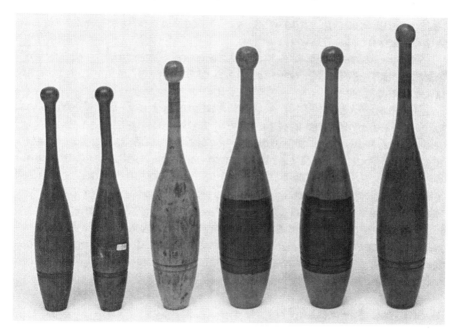

Swinging Clubs

Thus, then, you will do well to commence by swinging a pair of Indian clubs. This will loosen the shoulder-joints, expand and open the chest, giving the lungs plenty of room in which to play, and strengthen the wrists. It will also develop and harden the muscles of the biceps and forearm, and also those of the breast and at the back of the shoulder blades. It is a great mistake to have the clubs too heavy. For a novice I should recommend only two or three pounds, while even for old hands and professionals from five to seven pounds are heavy enough. Little benefit is derived by aimlessly swinging clubs without rule or method, but two or three regular evolutions should be learnt, and the exercise taken for about ten or fifteen minutes every morning, desisting from each evolution on the first feeling of requiring any extra strain to execute it.

The best motions are those known as "Windmill," "Moulinet," "Horizontal," and other combinations of the "inner" and "outer" front and back circles.

The correct position to stand when you are swinging clubs is as follows, remembering that what you want most is to see that your body and shoulders are equally square to the front: The heels should be exactly in a line and pretty close together, so that you can stand perfectly upright with ease and comfort. Turn the toes outward to form an angle of fifty or sixty degrees. Let the arms hang naturally and easily close to the side. Throw the body slightly forward so that the weight of it may be principally on the balls of the feet. Keep the head erect, the chin slightly drawn in toward the neck, and look straight in front of you, never letting your eyes follow the movement of the clubs.

Dumb-Bell Exercise

Laying aside the clubs, and after a couple of minutes' rest, take a turn at the dumb-bells. The weight of these most never be over a pound each, for in boxing, rapidity of movement is the essential to be aimed at, so do not attempt to handle any dumb-bells that make the motions slow and labored. The evolutions practiced should be those that open the chest, such as the second and third exercises of the "extension motions" in use in the army. Do not be led into hitting out from the shoulder with dumb-bells, no matter how light they may be, as it has a tendency to shorten your reach, besides being likely to severely wrench the elbow or shoulder-joints if you lunge out too freely. The best exercise with the dumb-bells and the one that occupies most of the attention of the professional boxer, is hitting out rapidly and continuously with both hands in rapid succession. This motion must be repeated over and over again many times every turn you take with the dumb-bells, and you should increase the duration of this exercise at each practice. This portion of your preparation exercises should not occupy more than 12 to 15 minutes.

The professional will do well to practice with the dumb-bells three or four times during the day, for periods not exceeding five minutes each bout, especially if he be in training for any special contest.

Punching the Bag

With every boxing man "punching the bag," as it is familiarly known, should occupy much time and careful attention. It is the only way that rapidity and smartness in hitting can be obtained. There are three different kinds of bags in use, of which the first is the heavy, weighing from ten to twenty pounds, swung from the ceiling by a strong rope, and covered by a thick wrapper of chamois-skin or soft kid, the inner stuffing being made of horse-hair. The method of its use is this: Give it a good swing to start it (for it should never be struck while motionless), then follow it rapidly about, hitting at it smartly and straight from the shoulder with the fists. Never hit the heavy bag as it is coming to you, as it would be very apt to dislocate the wrist, but catch it as it swings away from you, and drive it away at a tangent. This exercise is very arduous and fatiguing to a beginner, and if the heavy bag be used at all, it should be indulged in only after you have made some progress in the science of boxing and are familiar with the two lighter bags. As a matter of fact, the heavy bag is not greatly in vogue, even among professionals, and may be dispensed with by amateurs. Do not put on the gloves for punching the bag, but use the bare knuckles. If at first they should get a little raw or rubbed, a few applications of weak tannic acid solution, or rosin, or good strong pickle out of the salt-pork barrel, will soon make the hands and knuckles tough. If you do not care to disfigure the

hands, wear a very loose pair of kid or buckskin gloves in which you can tightly close the fists.

The Flying Bag

The next is the light swinging or "flying" bag. It is a large, inflated rubber bag pendant from the ceiling, if that be low enough to allow your hitting it up against it so that its return to your reach may be almost instantaneous. If the ceiling be too high, hang it in some convenient corner of the room, so that you can drive it hard and rapidly against the two walls. The great object to be aimed at is to make its return to you as quick as possible. In your bout with this imaginary enemy, who, being powerless to retaliate, must perforce fly from every blow, be careful always to assume the correct boxing position, which will be explained later.

Hit straight and sharp from the shoulder, letting the whole weight of your body follow the blow, so as to add weight and force to it. Strike rapidly with the right and left indiscriminately, according to the side on which the bag flies past you. If you are in real earnest with the fun, you will have all you can do following it round and about. It is splendid exercise for the legs, and the agility and quickness of getting about after the bag which, the exercise teaches, will

be a material benefit to you when facing an adversary. You should always keep your face to the bag; never let it for an instant fly behind your back, and remember that every time you miss it in its lightning-like gyrations, and every time it succeeds in eluding your blow and thumps you rudely on the chest, back, or face, it shows you that a more strenuous and electric rapidity of movement is required on your part.

The third bag is the one most generally in use, because it does not require so much room to be set up and less moving about getting after it. It is an oval bag three or four times the size of a Rugby football inflated with air, but instead of hanging loose it has a rope attached to the lower end securing it in a perpendicular position to the floor, as well as to the ceiling. Sometimes the upper and lower fastenings are made of thick rubber bands, which, of course, give a more rapid rebound to it when struck. The exercise with it is almost identical with that of the "flying" bag, but, as I said before, it does not run you round so much.

The Correct Position

As we have had occasion already to mention the act of striking, we shall now describe the position to be taken when standing up for a turn with the gloves. Of course, the rules laid down here are not to be taken too arbitrarily, but as your success will depend largely upon a position in which you can make use of your powers of attack and defense, and at the same time move with rapidity and decision, the general pose should conform to the important principles laid down. Stand, therefore, erect, with the head very slightly

thrown back; keep your mouth shut, with the tongue well behind the teeth; you should breathe only through the nose; a gapping mouth and lolling head are invariable signs of failing wind and general fatigue. Look your man full in the eye, and don't lose his gaze for an instant, for it is the infallible mirror which will inform you of what his brain is evolving before his limbs have time to execute it. Remember always that the left hand is the weapon of assault, the right being held for purposes of defense, or occasionally used for severe and crushing punishment. Of course, this remark does not imply that you are never to let drive with left and right in rapid succession, which is often done when opportunity offers, especially when you have to resort to "infighting," but it is laid down as a broad maxim, and should be followed when you are "out-sparring." Advance your *left* foot forward, therefore, planting it flat and firmly on the ground, and pointing in the direction of your opponent's left toe. The right foot should be about 10 to 14 inches in the rear of the left. In this separating of the feet be guided by your own inclinations and general habit, only don't stand with legs so widely sprawled apart as to impede the rapidity of your movements, or jeopardize the stability of the body. A good distance for a man of five feet five inches to five feet nine or 10 inches in height would be from 10 to 14 inches between the feet. For taller men the distance would be proportionately wider. Your main weight should now rest on the forward foot, and the right heel will be slightly raised from the ground, and only the ball of the foot touching. Many will tell you that both knees should be slightly bent, but it is by no means necessary - in fact, so long as you feel perfectly at ease and comfortable, make the most of your inches and stand bolt upright, but don't be stiff or rigid. A short man, by standing well up on his toes, can often get on equal terms with a man some inches his superior in height, to say nothing of the immense advantage it adds to his reach.

Shut the fists fairly close, even when sparring with the gloves on. Nothing is to be condemned so much as sparring open-handed, or with fingers only half shut. Serious accidents often result to the joints of the fingers from this stupid practice. How can you hit a clean, sharp blow straight out from the shoulder and land full on your adversary's person, without damaging your fingers, if open? If you think it too much like real fighting to close the fist when the gloves are on you had better take the gloves off and shake "the bones" for exercise. But let me, at the outset, warn you against keeping the fists tightly clenched all the time you are sparring, for it is a great strain on the muscles to be kept on protracted tension, and wears out the strength you ought to reserve for your blows. Let the fists be lightly closed when you are sparring round, but tighten them simultaneously with delivering your blow, or as you ward off your adversary's. This seems, perhaps, a slight point to stickle for, but a very short experience will show you its wisdom and importance when put into practice.

Raise your right forearm from the elbow and throw it across the chest so that the middle joint of the thumb, when shut on the fingers, is about the region of the nipple of the left breast, and its direction runs along the right "divide" of the ribs. The spot from whence the ribs branch off the breastbone to either side is generally known as "the mark," and is the most vulnerable of all the region below the neck. Let the whole arm hang easily from the shoulder and keep it just ever so slightly touching the right side. Raise the left arm now, with the knuckles of the fist at right angles with the ground and parallel with the body, and advance it forward and point the fist a trifle upward till the upper and lower portions of the arm form an angle of about 120°. Drop the elbow well into the side. Let the head be, if anything, a trifle inclined to the right and do not protrude the chin.

Although both eyes should look straight into those of your opponent, the left cheek should be rather more presented to him than the right, in order to prevent a blow at the *eyes* taking equally bad effect on both.

Walking and Running Exercise

A good long swinging walk should follow the indoor exercises. Not a loafing saunter, mind you, but a fair and square "heel and toe" four-mile-an-hour pace for at least a couple of hours. Of course, I am presuming that you have the time at your disposal, but if you have not, why, then take as much walking in the morning as you conveniently can, remembering always so to arrange the exercise that you will not be obliged to sit down all aglow from the exertion, because it stiffens the limbs very much to have the body cool off while seated perfectly still.

If going into regular training, or if you are past the halcyon days of five and twenty or thereabouts, and find you have a tendency to "put on flesh," the walk will have to be alternated by an occasional run of a couple of miles at a fair jog-trot, and if it is necessary to "fine down" considerably, you may be forced to run and walk in heavy "sweaters." If you are out of condition and perspire very freely, remember to rub down with a coarse towel until you are perfectly dry; and that to be sponged off with alcohol, or with any cheap, raw spirit, is also a great comfort and refreshment for weary limbs.

A word, here, of advice to brother professionals who will doubt-less be accompanied by the trainer at these exercises. Be sure and secure the services of a thoroughly competent and reliable man well up in the work he undertakes for you, and who will spare no pains to get you into the best trim possible. It is better to pay twice as much to a really good man that knows his business than a small sum to an inferior man who knows no more than you do. My remarks, of course, do not intend to refer to old pugilists who, by long experience, know just as well as any trainer how to take exercise, and only require a good, strong, willing friend along to rub them down, but to the novice who is in training possible for his first battle or for a contest with the gloves, Queensbury rules. A good man always costs less money in the end.

Should these exertions create an unnatural feeling of lassitude, and having done more than you can recover from for the rest of the day, it is permissible to drink a small glass of weak spirits and water, but as a general rule the maxim is, abstain from spirits alto-gether as being too heating to the blood; and, if you can do so with-out distressing yourself, do not drink even water between meals. If really thirsty, suck the juice of a lemon a little, but do not load your stomach with effervescing drinks like ginger ale, lemonade, etc., and be not deluded into the habit of swallowing raw eggs, or imbib-ing seductive spoonfuls of egg whipped in sherry, or the like, for such stimulants are only a snare and an abomination to the really sound and robust constitution, and are no aid in building up a weak one.

Dinner Diet

Noontide should find you rested and refreshed, with a decided hankering after the call of the dinner bell. And let me remind you again before commencing your meal, beware of "slops"; therefore eschew rich and greasy soups (I know you'll say that soups ought not to be greasy, but nevertheless they oft times are). But half a dozen raw oysters, or clams, make an excellent beginning, and give you an appetite for what's to follow. You may eat very nearly anything you fancy, flesh being, of course, preferred to fowl, and under-done to well-done meats. Of vegetables be sparing, but a lit-tle spinach, cabbage, beetroot, or turnip won't hurt you in ordinary

training, but must be totally discarded when preparing for a severe contest of any kind. But turn from the mealy potato, and regard not the flavor of snow-white rice. Eat heartily, but slowly and deliberately, don't bolt your foot, which is the chief root of indigestion, dyspepsia, heartburn, and a thousand other ills. You are at liberty to wash down your dinner with a tumbler of ale or a bottle of stout, but be moderate in your potations. If the sweet tooth of childhood still lingers in your mouth and you yearn for a top-dressing of pudding or pie, let it be light and plain, and not too much of it. If in for the strictest and hardest training, you must eat no sweets at all. Let the afternoon be devoted to quiet study, to business, or almost do just what you please in the way of work or play.

If you take your boxing lessons in the afternoon, let them not commence till at least three hours after dinner, and before going to your lesson or putting the gloves on with a friend, have a five minutes' "go in" at the bag, which will just limber up things beautifully. If the professional be training for a battle in the prize ring, or for a severe glove contest, let him be guarded against boxing with any other person but his trainer; because it might happen that his intended adversary, learning the fact, and finding out who the men are, would take means to secure such to inflict intentional damage to him by foul play or otherwise. So I repeat the caution against:

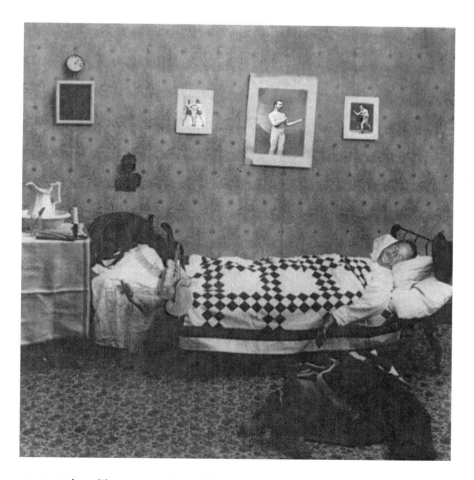

spar only with your trainer. When you have the gloves on, go into the exercise heart and soul, and spar quick and strong, but don't let the round exceed four minutes; if you've been doing all you know, four minutes will seem mighty long in coming, and the minute's rest will be but as 15 seconds. Three good rounds should be a feast for a glutton, and enough to keep up your science, your health, and your love of the sport. More than that would make work of what ought to be in reality a pleasure.

Before retiring for the night, which should always be at the same hour, swing your clubs and use your dumb-bells for about half as long as you do in the morning, but at least half an hour should elapse after the exercise before you turn in. A light rubdown with the palm of the hand before jumping into bed will sweeten slumber, and you will sleep, if not the sleep of the just, at least the sleep of the healthy.

PART THREE
THE ART OF BOXING

ENTERING THE RING

Having, then, by the course of training and exercise previously prescribed, prepared yourself to undergo the violent exertion that boxing, but more especially *learning* to box, entails, you will be naturally eager to commence the exhilarating enjoyment of the sport. But, before "facing your man," there are several little points that it is always well to bear in mind, and by the observance of which you will materially strengthen your probabilities of success.

In every case, therefore, where it is by any means feasible, let your lessons with the teacher, or your practice bouts with friends, be taken in the open air, rather than in the close confinement of a covered building. You cannot have a finer arena than a nice, springy, level plot of close green turf; but if you are obliged to box in a hall, or in your own room, see that all the windows and doors are wide open, and that there is plenty of ventilation, and a free circulation of fresh air. This fact is more particularly necessary if you spar at night, by gaslight, for burning lights consume a great deal of the life-giving oxygen in the atmosphere, and the process of combustion generates a continued supply of that most noxious of all gases, the deadly carbonic acid. To breath this gas even in the smallest quantities when the body is not undergoing any exertion, and when, therefore, the poison can only enter through the lungs, is depressing; but when inhaled more copiously by rapid panting and also absorbed by the pores of the skin, opened by exercise, like so many thousands of tiny mouths, to take it in, carbonic acid is seriously detrimental to the free action of the heart and lungs, and quickly produces a feeling of suffocation, headache, and nausea.

Don't box in your shirtsleeves, or any such loose garment; and don't wear braces or the like support for your trousers. Don a close-fitting, elastic jersey, cut very short in the sleeves, or better still, with no sleeves at all, so that the arm and shoulder can play perfectly free and untrammeled. Always be careful and wear boots that are a firm, strong support to the ankles. If you are sparring on the greensward, a light pair of high-laced, or elastic-side walking-boots are the proper thing, but they should have at least three good spikes securely fastened to the sole of the boot, as, without these supports, you are apt to slip and slide about when attempting to move suddenly and rapidly.

The regulations of the London Prize Ring Rules require "That the spikes in the fighting boots shall be confined to *three* in number, which shall not exceed three-eights of an inch from sole of the boot, and shall not be less than one-eight of an inch broad at the point; two to be placed in the broadest part of the sole, and one on the heel; and that in the event of a man's wearing any other spikes, either in the toes or elsewhere, he shall be compelled either to remove them, or provide other boots properly spiked, the penalty for refusal to be a loss of the stakes."

When on boards, lighter boots, with canvas uppers, are used, but the soles are of rubber. But discard the low-cut shoe. The head should never be covered indoors or out - not even by the flimsiest of caps.

The Ring and Ground

It is generally customary to spar in a 24-foot rectangular space, technically termed "the ring," on the *lucus à non lucendo* principle, that it never is circular. Sometimes, from want of space, or by previous arrangement, a smaller ring of only eighteen feet is the allotted ground; and I have known instances of the ring being only twelve feet square, but this is really too small for the essentials of learning to spar, and leads to a great deal of "hammer-and-tongs" hitting, hugging, and "in-fighting" which ought to be avoided. Of course, in boxing for pleasure, we need not be governed by any prescribed limits; only, to dance round a 10-acre lot for fear of coming to close quarters is not what is generally understood by boxing; but just bear in mind that nine times out of 10 when you get mixed up in a row or street fight, and your knowledge of how to handle your fists comes into play, you will find yourself jammed into a tight place, and, more likely than not, have no room to spar round and

round your man; so my advice to you is, learn to move smartly about in as small a space as possible; and then just think what a saving of wind and legs and energy it is!

The particulars as regards the proper pitching of the ring, the positions and corners allotted to the combatants, and the other details that govern a prize ring contest, are given in the London Prize Ring Rules, printed at the end of this treatise.

The Ring

As you enter "the ring" it is a good old English custom to go up and shake your adversary heartily with the gloved hand, and I think that is a capital way even for friends, or pupil and teacher, to open the bout. But as you do so keep your eyes open, and on your man; take in his height; just the length of his arm; run him all over and see if he looks in as good condition as you are; for on these impressions will your tactics mainly depend. If your opponent be heavier or taller than yourself, you will naturally say, "I must be wary not to let him get at too close quarters with me often." If he seems a trifle stout or in bad condition, you will mentally observe,

"I'll rush you round a bit, you fine fellow; you shall have plenty of exercise before I've done with you." Immediately after you have relinquished your opponent's hand, step briskly back a couple of paces and throw yourself at once into your posture of defense.

Advancing and Breaking Ground

Now I want every one who intends to profit by these simple lessons, to pay particular heed to what is said about being able to get about smartly on one's legs, for no amount of skill and activity with the hands will counteract the grievous fault of being slow in moving your feet. Of the two things I think it is less of a disadvantage to be slow with the hands than slow on the feet. In the one case you may not be able to punish your man as quickly or as often as he may perhaps deserve, but on the other hand, slow feet will infallibly let you in for many a heavy blow that activity of movement would enable you to escape.

Don't, therefore, stand with your legs stretched widely apart; it is bound to make you unsteady, slow, and awkward, besides taking considerably from your height, of which you ought to make the most. If, again, you stand with your feet too close together, you are very apt to hitch one in the other and stumble and give your adversary a chance that he will be only too ready to seize. How often have I heard men say when looking on at an amateur performance with the gloves, "By Jove! That fellow's feet are always getting in his way," or, "The only trouble with him is, he can't get out of the way of his own feet." Don't hazard any such occasion for remark in your case. Plant the left foot firmly and squarely on the ground, and let the heel be from 12 to 16 inches in front of, and at right angles to, your right foot. A line drawn along the center of the left foot should cut another along the right about the hollow of the foot and nearly at right angles.

In advancing never put the right foot before the left, as in walking, but let the right follow the left and fall Just about on the place where the left was raised form. That is to say, in progression and retrogression your legs should always be about as far apart as they usually are when standing on guard. In the technical language of the ring, the motion of retreat is known as "breaking ground," and should always be performed by first moving the right foot backward

BOTH ON GUARD - Billy Edwards on the left and Arthur Chambers on the right (This cut shows the correct positions of the hands, and the proper distance that the feet should be kept while sparring.)

and then drawing the left foot back to the place originally occupied by the right. To "break ground," therefore, is to retire; so if you "break ground" to the right, it means that you are working backward, but at the same time moving toward your right, and consequently passing more to your adversary's left. In "breaking ground" to the left, the right foot is moved backward and to the left, followed by the left foot working always in front, but toward the left.

Both on Guard

On coming into sparring distance of your adversary you will find that you are close enough when your left fist, held as previously explained, is about level with his wrist. Your left toe will be 15 to 18 inches from his left. In sparring for an opening to hit, be very quick, easy, and free in all your movements. Don't make play with the hands alone, but let the feet and body follow in unison with the movement of the hands. When you make up your mind to hit, do so clean and straight from the shoulder, and with lightning rapidity, advancing the left foot as you deliver the blow, and adding the whole weight of your body in the lunge forward. The greatest care should always be taken not to hit out fiercely when out of distance, which you should always calculate most accurately, for there is nothing that so jars the muscles of the arm as striking out and only "beating the air," and finding no material resistance. Not but what many of your blows will be avoided by ducking or "side-slipping," but this you will be more or less prepared for; but what you must guard against is, hitting out and *overreaching.* As a rule, don't deal any blows by swinging the arms like a windmill. I know you will often hear so-called experts talk loudly about how cleverly so-and-so "swings his right." This is all very well, and there are instances when, as a proficient, you will readily learn to "swing," and with crushing effect, but be satisfied at first to spar straight from the shoulder, whether hitting with the right or the left.

Sparring Round, Feinting, and Drawing

In sparring round your man keep the left foot and hand well in front of you, and after delivering a blow take ground to the right, for by so doing you are working away from his punishing arm, the right. But should you hit and dodge to the left, you will find he will be "propping" you heavily with his right in a way that will soon teach you better.

It may be very reasonably asked, Why is it necessary to stand with the *left* arm and *left* foot advanced and not allow a man to fall into the position which he would naturally take to strike a blow, if he knew nothing about boxing, that is, with the right fist? The reason is, that long experience has proved that by teaching the novice to stand with the *left* arm and foot in front is the only way in which he can be given the same free facility in the use of either hand. That is to say, the constant use of his *left* hand for striking makes him ambidextrous. Moreover, it should be always borne in mind that it holds the right hand in reserve in case a chance occur to give your antagonist the *coup de grace*.

A feint is a ruse by which you divert your opponent's attention from the real object of your attack by pretending to deal a blow

BOTH ON GUARD (alternate view) - Arthur Chambers on the left and Billy Edwards on the right.

which you do not fully carry out. Thus, if your real intention be to strike a body blow with your right, hit out smartly but lightly with your left; he will as quickly raise his right arm to catch your blow, when you will in a flash dash in your right heavily on the pit of the stomach, at the same time keeping an eye on what he is about with his own right. I ought, by the way, to have said that in guarding all blows endeavor to catch them on the muscles of the back or front of the forearm, and glance the blow off with a slanting arm; and do not, if you can help it, allow the fist to fall on the bone, for a down-right hard blow on the bone may break it. This very accident happened in one of the early rounds of the immortal set-to between Sayers and Heenan, when the little Englishman fought for over an hour with his right arm disabled by a blow from his gigantic antagonist.

By "drawing" is meant that opportunity you purposely give your

THE DOUBLE LEAD AND STOP - Arthur Chambers on left, Billy Edwards on right. Both hit out simultaneously with their left and catch the blow on right arm.

adversary by laying yourself open to a certain blow which you feel sure he is bound to try and get in, in order that you may, while avoiding it, deal another, which he will then give you the chance to do. To do this cleverly and with effect requires a cool head, keen judgment, and an immense amount of practice, and, to the uninitiated, is more often attempted with disastrous results rather than with success. Yet. It looks pretty and so easy, and gains you such "gallery" when it comes off, that it is too often made use of. So my advice to the beginner would be, don't try it on till you've become an old hand at the gloves, and not even then unless you are sure you know a good deal more than the man you are boxing with.

THE DOUBLE LEAD AND STOP (alternate view) - Billy Edwards on left, Arthur Chambers on right. Both hit out with the left fist and catch the blow on right arm.

The Double Lead and Stop

This is really about the first evolution that you ought to master, as among the ordinary run of boxing men it is the usual way of opening. It is thus performed: Lead off with the left at the head at precisely the same moment your adversary leads his left at your head, at the same time throwing up your right, or guard arm, to catch the blow. In putting your right arm, be careful not to obstruct your own line of sight, for you should never for an instant lose his eye. Try and catch the blow on the fleshy part of the arm by the elbow, and watch him over your wrist. It will of course be readily understood that before this opening blow is struck, both men have feinted and sparred for an opening. Other opening blows, such as feelers on the ribs and chest, are also very common.

The Straight, or Simple Counter

The straight counter takes place when both men lead off at the head at the same time, and do not attempt to guard the blow with the right arm, so that each blow takes effect on the face. In making this blow, swing your body in with the fist and turn your head slightly over the right shoulder, so that your cheek shall receive the blow rather than his glove should encounter your eyes, nose, or mouth.

THE STRAIGHT COUNTER - Billy Edwards on left, Arthur Chambers on right. Both hit out with left, and land on the other's left cheek.

THE DUCK FORWARD, BY BILLY EDWARDS - Billy Edwards on left, Arthur Chambers on right.

Ducking

As a great many of the blows aimed at the head may be successfully avoided by a slight by timely movement of that most important member, and at the same time leave both your hands free for attack, or to defend some other part that is assailed at the same moment, it is most necessary to acquire, at an early period of your lessons, the useful art of "ducking." There are three distinct movements of the head known as "ducking":

1. To the right, when the head is thrown quickly on to the *right* shoulder, allowing a blow aimed at it to pass by your *left* ear.
2. To the left, which permits the blow to glance over the *right* ear.
3. When the head is lowered and thrown forward, so as to allow the blow to pass harmlessly over it.

To perform this delicate maneuver adroitly, everything must depend upon the accuracy with which it is timed, for if you incline your head to the right or left a moment too soon, your adversary has time, so to alter the direction of the blow, that it falls upon the unprotected neck, which is a most severe shock, and on that you will not care to have repeated. Be very careful, also, while ducking, to keep your eyes on your man all the time, and more particularly when you are ducking forward; and while in this position, remember not to raise the head again before you "break ground" out of his reach. Don't forget, too, that while the primary effect of the "duck" is to enable you to avoid your opponent's blow, it should always afford you the opportunity of delivering one yourself. Never duck, therefore, without hitting a blow at the same time. If you are fighting a man considerably taller than yourself, you will find it a capital chance to get in some telling body blows. These body blows always have the effect of making a man careful how he lunges out from the shoulder and leaves his ribs uncovered. When you duck to the right, hit with the left hand at head or body. If you duck to the

THE DUCK AND BODY BLOW - Chambers on left, Edwards on right. Chambers has ducked blow by Edwards' left, and puts in a body-blow with left at Edwards.

left, you will probably get a chance to cross-counter with your right at either face or chest.

Guards

Very much depends upon your knowing how to ward off, or at least mitigate the full force of such blows as you cannot easily duck from, and also blows on the body, which, if not properly guarded, would soon knock all the breath out of you, no matter how well you may be trained, or however good condition you may be in. I will, therefore, now proceed to enumerate most of the essential guards, and explain how each is generally performed. As there are in reality but four distinct blows made use of in boxing, namely:

1. Left hand at the head
2. Left-hand body blow
3. Right hand at the head
4. Right-hand body blow

so there must also be four recognized guards for these blows. And I may as well explain here the difference between a "stop" and guarding. By the later term is meant receiving your adversary's blow on the right or left arm as the emergency demands; but a "stop" technically speaking, is planting some sudden blow which prevents the hit intended by your opponent from reaching its destination. For example, at the instant you see your antagonist intends to deliver a body blow with his left which would necessitate your dropping your right across "the mark" to catch it, you anticipate his blow by dashing your left full into his face and catching him on the forehead before he can get his head down, which would naturally be his position when he comes in to deliver the blow. Your right arm remains, of course, in its natural position. I have already explained the method of guarding the left-hand head-blow, so let us proceed to the left-hand blow at the body.

You must bear in mind that a blow delivered by your opponent's *left* hand at your body will fall on your left chest or side. Therefore it will be your left hand that must be used as a guard in this instance. Put up your right arm immediately and at the same time drop your left across the "mark," keeping the elbow well into the side, and the whole of the forearm braced firmly against the ribs, because if the left arm be out a little distance from the side, and be driven by your adversary's blow hard against your body, the sudden jar is very apt to knock a good bit of wind out of you. As you receive the blow, "break ground" a little in case he should follow the blow up with a rush.

And here let me give you a most important piece of advice. Never rush at a man furiously or blindly with your head down because you think he is shirking you, and you are in a hurry to go in and finish him up. In the first place you can't see what you are about, and you get within his reach, giving him an opportunity of letting you have his right and left, or, as is often called, "the postman's rap," several times before you can recover yourself and get out of the way. In the second, it brings about a great deal of "infighting," which, though you have often to resort to if caught in a rough-and-tumble scrimmage, is not considered quite the thing when gentlemen are sparring for fun and pleasure. Therefore I say, avoid frantic rushing, but follow up an advantage quickly yet deliberately.

The usual guard for a right-hand blow at the head is thus effected: Raise the left elbow sharply, pointing it somewhat in the direction of the coming blow, at the same time drop the left fist in toward the body, the palm being slightly turned from you. Lean forward and catch the blow close by the elbow, on the forearm, and retire slightly directly you feel the full brunt of it, watching your man the while over the lowered wrist. The guard for the right-hand body-blow is, to drop the left hand almost to its full length, so that your fist falls on the inner side of the left thigh, and the same moment, raising the shoulder smartly up toward the chin and rounding it and the whole upper arm forward on to the chest, and *slightly* turning the left side of the body. Brace all the muscles by tightly clenching the fist, and keep the whole arm firmly pressed against the side. This position, properly taken, should shield the heart and the whole of the left side of the body.

Countering

Countering is a term which, in sparring, has reference to delivering a blow to your adversary at the precise moment he hits you, or you avoid his lead by ducking, or otherwise. There are two kinds of counters: the simple or straight counter, and the cross-counter - the latter being, when cleverly administered, perhaps the most deadly and effective blow that can be struck in boxing. A left-hand counter is delivered by ducking to the *right*, so as to allow your opponent's left-hand lead at the head to pass over your left shoulder, and stepping in a good pace with the left foot and letting drive your left full in his face, immediately drawing the foot back upon planting the blow. When you are at "out-sparring" this blow tells splendidly, and if you are quick and active on your legs, you can, if you are smart enough, keep tap, tap, tapping a duffer or slow-coach without his ever being able to get at you to return the compliment. The same blow can be struck by guarding the head instead of ducking, and at the same time hitting out as directed.

THE RIGHT-HAND CROSS-COUNTER, BY ARTHUR CHAMBERS - Chambers on left, Edwards on right. Edwards leads with left. Chambers avoids blow by right side slip of head, at same time plants blow on Edwards' left jaw, with the right fist crossing over Edwards' left.

THE RIGHT-HAND CROSS-COUNTER, BY BILLY EDWARDS - Chambers leads with left. Edwards eludes by head side-slip to right, at the same time plants blow on Chambers' left jaw, by hitting with right over Chambers' left.

Right-hand Cross-Counter

The right-hand cross-counter is delivered by stepping in ten to fifteen inches as your opponent leads off at the head and while "getting in" ducking smartly to the *left*; turn your body toward your man so as to bring the right arm well up, and shoot it out over his outstretched left. Your blow will naturally take rather an upward tendency, and should be aimed at the angle of the jaw or the chin, and your fist will perform a quarter circle to the left, and should reach the face with its palm turned to the ground. To perform this rightly requires the utmost nicety and accuracy in timing yourself, and then hand, eye, foot, and body must work in perfect unison, and all move with the rapidity of lighting. To master it, time, skill, and constant, unremitting practice are required, but to attain it scientifically put forth your very best endeavors, for not a blow or guard in boxing will repay you more than the cross-counter, which may well be called the sheet-anchor of the science.

THE HEAD SLIP AND BODY BLOW - Chambers on the left, Edwards on the right. Chambers leads left at head, Edwards eludes by head-slip to right, at the same time landing on Chambers' ribs with his left.

Body Blows - Right and Left

Although the main point of attack must always be the face and head of your opponent, yet you should never neglect an opportunity to get in frequent and heavy blows about the chest and pit of the stomach, for these hits, when sent home, are sure to tell in the long run, and often are more efficacious in breaking up your antagonist's wind than the severer punishment you inflict on his upper story.

The openings you will be offered for hitting at the body will generally be when your adversary is leading off at your own head with either the right or left hand. When he does so, instead of ducking or guarding and returning the counter at the head, a retaliation on your part he will more than likely expect, and be, therefore, prepared for, you will return on the body. But let me caution you first and always to see that you have plenty of room behind you for retreat before you step in to deliver a body blow, which will neces-

THE HEAD SLIP AND BODY BLOW - Edwards on the left, Chambers on the right. Edwards leads with the left. Chambers eludes by head slip to right, and at the same time lands with the left on Edwards' body.

sitate you going in much closer to your man than when you are making play at his face. The blow should be aimed as much as possible at the opening of the ribs, for that is the most vulnerable part of the lower target. If you intend, then, having a "go" at the body, it is often good to feint a lead-ff at the head, as this will cause him to throw up his right arm to guard; as he does so step in very quickly about a couple of feet with the left foot, and the same moment letting drive your left with all your might at the uncovered "mark," and ducking well to the right, so that if your opponent "counters" with his left, you'll be out of his reach. Spring back immediately you have ducked to the counter. The principal thing you have to guard against in attempting this blow is, that your adversary anticipates it and strikes you full in the face with the left before you have time to get your head down.

In delivering a right-hand body blow you will have to be a good deal closer in to your man than is the case when hitting with the left, so you will not need to take so long a stride when striking. The blow is generally aimed at the heart, and is much the same as the one just described, only be sure you duck to the left instead of to the right. Hence, from the above we formulate a very simple rule, and one that can be easily kept in the head: Lead with left, duck to right; lead with right, duck to left.

Upper Cuts - Right and Left

These most unpleasant surprises are generally given when your opponent, in his endeavor to get in a body blow, lunges forward, and in consequence has his head thrown well in front of the body, and his forehead bent toward the ground. Whenever you see your adversary's head down, no matter what his reason for it may be, be ready with an "upper cut." The blow is given thus: Drop your left fist somewhat and draw the whole arm as far back as you can,

THE RIGHT-HAND UPPER CUT - Edwards on the left, Chambers on the right. Chambers leads left at Edwards' head, lurching head forwards with the blow. Edwards eludes by head-slip to right, at the same moment delivering the "upper cut" with right.

THE RIGHT-HAND UPPER CUT - Chambers on the left, Edwards on the right. Edwards leads left at Chambers' head, throwing his head forward with the blow. Chambers eludes by head-slip to right, delivering right-hand "upper cut" at same time.

then swing it up like lightning, so as to go between your opponent's hands, and land under his chin or on his mouth, or, if you are a little too far off for that, to lift him on the nose or forehead. This blow cannot be given from the shoulder direct, and you must help it by swinging your body upward, as it were. If a clever man is in front of you beware how you attempt the "upper cut," because he throws his head forward, for it is one of the most ingenious methods of "drawing" you to try it, so that by ducking right he can get in a heavy left-hand body blow. You must, therefore, learn to discriminate very carefully between a *bona fide* overreach, causing the head to lurch forward, and the artful "draw."

The Side Step

There is no maneuver in the whole art of boxing that is so timely and useful as the one known as "sideslipping." It is generally resorted to in avoiding your antagonist's most furious rushes, especially if he is a good deal heavier man than you are, and comes in at you constantly to force you to "in-fighting." To be able to perform it at a moment's notice you must be particularly quick on your feet, and have your legs completely under the most perfect control. It will be the means of getting you out of many a tight fix when driven too near the edge of the ropes or into a corner, and if you can perform it spontaneously, will save you much exertion and help you to keep your wind, as, after performing it successfully, you can generally catch a moment's respite before your man faces you again after dashing past you. You will also find that it often happens that the impetus of his rush which you elude by "side-slipping" will make him stagger forward, perhaps ever so slightly, but during that precious moment you can swing in a heavy blow with the left or right, which will complete his total overthrow.

Lose no opportunity of practicing it, both when exercising in your room, and when taking a turn with the gloves. This is the way in which it is done: Make a pretense of standing up to your man

THE SIDE STEP - Edwards left, Chambers right. Edwards following up, Chambers gets out of reach by the side step.

THE SIDE STEP - Chambers left, Edwards right. Chambers following up, Edwards gets out of reach by side step to left.

and feint to strike at him either on the chest or arm, but do not "break ground," and as he takes his next step in, duck smartly to the right, make a rapid movement, half step, half jump, half run, passing nimbly under his left arm, and face him instantly by turning sharply to your left. If done rapidly, you should be by him, and have turned in time to see the back of his shoulder. But in doing this keep the head well turned to the left, and never have your eyes off him for a single moment. Nothing but constant practice will enable you to time the side jump accurately, and a flash of hesitation while in the execution of it will be awfully fatal.

In-Fighting

It only remains for me to say a word or two relative to "in-fighting," which perhaps ought not to be included in a description of sparring pure and simple; but as it often happens that two friends,

IN-FIGHTING - Edwards left, Chambers right. Edwards gets both hands inside those of Chambers and makes play at the head, Chambers forced to strike at the body.

evenly matched, get warmed up to the work, and when at close quarters will go it hammer and tongs for a couple of seconds, without very great harm coming of it, I may as well show that there is a method even in this set-to when no guarding, feinting, or ducking can be done, and when everything depends on the rapidity and precision with which the arms are used. It generally takes place in a corner of the ring, or at the edge of one of the sides, and results from the fact that the man who is forcing his antagonist back has been too close after him or too quick to allow him to get away by "side-slipping," and intends to force "in-fighting." If, then, you are caught in this predicament (which, by the way, is just what happens in a general street row), stand up square, bringing up the right foot and right shoulder; let the heels be pretty even and about a foot apart; slightly bend both knees; drop your chin well down into your throat and lean forward. Keep your eyes open; no amount of blows must cause you to shut them in this extremity. If you do you are lost

IN-FIGHTING - Chambers left, Edwards right. Chambers gets both hands inside those of Edwards and makes play at the head, Edwards forced to strike at the body.

indeed. Strike out with right and left just as fast as you know how, but do not draw the fists farther back than the ribs, and swing the shoulder in with each blow. Make play at the face if you can, and keep the fists and arms close together, so that your opponent doesn't get a chance to get in between them. If you are so unfortunate as to let your adversary have the inner gauge of you and you can't get at his face, why, then all you can do is to get in all your work on his body, and be sure to let the blows go home hard and heavy. Of course, when "in-fighting" you will not choose to make play at the body rather than the head and face, but hit at the body rather than not hit at all.

After the Lesson

Strip and have a good rub down with a rough towel while you

are still aglow with perspiration, until you cool off and are perfectly dry. If you have chanced receive a blow that feels as if it will wear stiff, apply a little liniment, such as *Pond's Extract*, or give it a rubbing with arnica or *Colgate Vaseline*. If your body is sound and healthy and in good hard training, the hardest blow with the gloves will not raise any disfiguring bump. The gloves you use should not weight less than six to eight ounces, and be made of the very best soft white kid or chamois leather, fully and evenly stuffed, and should allow your fist to close easily, and when closed to completely envelop the whole hand; an elastic band should hold them firmly to the wrist.

We will now assume that the learner has become familiar with the different blows, stops, and guards that are of most importance in acquiring the art of self-defense; but in order to perfect himself scientifically in the practice of boxing, it is necessary that he master each evolution in detail, so as to execute it readily and easily at the instant the opportunity presents itself, without having to refer to the text-book of his memory before he can remember the correct guard or stop that should meet each onslaught of his adversary.

The First Lessons

The first lessons should be given slowly and deliberately by the teacher, taking each evolution in detail, and accompanying the practical demonstration of the particular maneuver by a running commentary of pertinent oral instruction, pointing out the precise object to be achieved, and reprimanding any fault of execution immediately on its occurrence, for by that means you keep the brain actively employed in harmonizing the uniformity of action, of eye, hand and foot.

By way of illustration, let us suppose that the left-hand lead at head and guard for the same with right is to be taught. The mode of instruction should run somewhat after this fashion: "Advance and lead as I lead." "That's too slow." "Quicker and straighter with the left." "Don't raise the right elbow so much. That's better; turn the right arm out a little more." "I'm going to follow up; break ground smartly to left." "Not such long strides; quicker." "Follow me up now." "There, never advance the right foot." "Now lead and get back. That's it; now then, quicker delivery," and so on. The exercise proceeds the whole time without intermission, the teacher increasing the celerity of action as the pupil gets more and more into the hang of the evolution, until the motion becomes almost involuntary, and is performed with the requisite velocity and with the rhythmic regularity of a pendulum. The pupil should never stop to argue or ask questions during the bout, but should, without opening his mouth, set his whole thoughts and energies to follow out each suggestion as it comes. He should pay close attention to the general style of his teacher's movements and endeavor to copy his general carriage, gaining that nameless something in grace and dexterity of the slightest movement that to the initiated eye infallibly indicates the proficient.

A round of this nature, which is begun deliberately, and does not call forth all the activity of a regular set-to, may be extended to five minutes or even a trifle longer, at the discretion of the teacher; but a change of exercise should not be commenced until the pupil shows himself master of the one he is engaged with.

Hard Hitting

Teachers should always be most careful, especially when

instructing their younger pupils, not to hit too hard, for a heavy blow to one unaccustomed to such sudden shocks is apt to confuse a novice so that he becomes incapable of fully comprehending the points that are verbally given. And besides this, rough treatment at the early stages of instruction implants a feeling of nervous excitement and general insecurity to avoid punishment, which militates much against that calm and cool-headed confidence that ought to be the first principle with which to inspire a beginner.

And in this connection, it may not be out of place to mention that no one who is aware that he is subject to any cardiac irregularity should attempt so severe a strain on that organ as is boxing. And so also he who has any pulmonary trouble should be very careful how he indulges in so boisterous a pastime, for an unexpected blow in the region of the lungs will often accelerate hemorrhages which may cause serious trouble afterward.

Right Arm and Foot in Front

Hitherto I have confined myself entirely to the practice of boxing by those who stand in the usual way, advancing the left foot and hand; but many men, either from preference, or because they have not be taught to box after the orthodox fashion, stand with the right leg in front, and hit with the right hand, using the left as the guard, and as no treatise on the subject can be said to be complete that does not tell you what to do when opposed to a man who faces you with the right hand in front, I shall proceed to discuss the general methods that are adopted. You may take comfort, though, from the fact that nine times out of ten the man that advances his right foot and hand does so because he is not accustomed to box, and being right-handed, naturally is more ready to deal blows with that hand than with the left. Such an opponent will not give you trouble, as you will easily not by the general position he assumes when approaching you whether he knows what he is about or not.

If, however, you find he is an old hand at the art, be careful not to let him get at very close quarters with you; and avoid leading at his head with your left, for this would be practically trying to cross-counter your left over his extended right, when he has not led at your head, and is, therefore, away beyond reach at which you could have any success in getting to him. No; rather let all your leads be given with your right hand, and if you duck from his right, remember to duck toward your *left* shoulder.

As he leads off at your head with the right, retaliate as if you were cross-countering a man in the usual position with your right. Be ready when he attempts right-hand body blows to land your left on his right jaw and neck. When you wish to make play at his body with the left, remember to get into hitting distance, as if you were before a man with left hand in front, and you intended attempting the right-hand body blow I have explained in a previous page. Guard his right-hand blows with your left, and his left-hand blows with your right.

The Clinch

I have already said that in usual sparring no such thing as hugging, holding, wrestling, or kicking should be permitted; but taking it for granted that having made yourself thoroughly at home with the regular methods, you are naturally anxious to know something about modes of fighting that are confined, I am happy to say, only to the prize ring proper, and the knowledge of which will often stand you in good stead at a pinch, I will lay them before you.

The "clinch" is often resorted to when one of the antagonists has suffered severe punishment at "infighting," and wishes to get away by closing and then pushing free. Or sometimes both are anxious to get a breathing spell after a fierce give and take, and lock to gain support and a moment or two's respite from hitting or being hit. Again, when a man has led and passed over his opponent's left shoulder, he will affect a clinch rather than incur the punishment he has laid himself open to. When you want to clinch, get very close in to your adversary; in fact, throw yourself bodily upon his chest, grasp his left elbow with your hand and hold it firmly against your body, or press it strongly against his. Hug him as closely as you can round the neck or body with the right, and above all, don't give him an opportunity to hit you with either hand. To break away from this contact, place your forearm against your adversary's throat and force back his head, at the same time freeing your other arm from his grasp, and plying him lustily with heavy body blows. After you get him at arm's length, don't let him have time to recover himself, but press him vigorously, and don't give

THE CLINCH - Chambers left, Edwards right. Chambers trying to hug, Edwards attempting to break away.

THE CLINCH - Edwards left, Chambers right. Edwards endeavoring to hold, Chambers trying to break away.

him the chance to close again.

In Chancery

I pity the poor wight that is so unfortunate as to get caught in such a predicament, but how to get him there I know not. No rule can be laid down, but in close quarters and at "in-fighting," opportunities present themselves, and the expert takes advantage of them. If you get the chance, fling your left arm round your adversary's neck, pull his head downward against your left side, hold him there and pummel away to your heart's content as long as he will let you. If you are fairly caught "in chancery," don't struggle to free yourself by pulling away, for by so doing you will only get strangled worse and worse; but push your opponent back with all your might, at the same time strike out vigorously with both hands, and try to trip him up by locking your leg behind his. When you think your opponent intends attempting "chancery," strike up his forearm under the elbow, at the same time ducking freely and breaking ground out of his reach.

IN CHANCERY - Chambers left, Edwards right. Chambers gets Edwards' head under his left arm, and punishes by upper cuts. Edwards tries to break away by body blows.

IN CHANCERY - Edwards left, Chambers right. Edwards gets Chambers' head under left arm, and punishes by upper cuts. Chambers is getting in body blows.

Back-Heeling

The two previous maneuvers, together with the two that follow, are admissible under the London Prize Ring Rules, but opportunities for making use of them are of very rare occurrence. Back-heeling, as the name implies, is a method of throwing your antagonist by the aid of tripping him over your heels. It differs but little from another method of throwing, known as *cross-buttock*, in which case the hip is used as the fulcrum upon which you lever over the body of your adversary.

If ever you are caught in any of these traps, look rather to your tumble than struggle to prevent it, for, the more desperate your efforts, so much the more severe will be your fall, because of the great strain and tension on all muscles at the moment of impact with the hard ground; but if you let yourself go limp, and rather assist than retard your fall, you are not liable to sustain half some much injury as when you fall while struggling to prevent it.

Much, very much, has been said against this truly manly and

BACK-HEELING - Edwards seizes Chambers around the neck with right arm, and throws him by using his right heel behind Chambers' left. (This is only allows by London P. R. Rules. Not admissible in Queensberry or Fair Play, which see.)

BACK-HEELING - Chambers seizes Edwards with right arm, and placing his left under Edwards' chin, forces him back by tripping him over with his left heel behind Edwards' left. (This is allowed in London P. R. Rules. Not admissible in Queensberry or Fair Play, which see.)

THE CROSS-BUTTOCK - Edwards left, Chambers right. Chambers throwing Edwards, by getting him across his hip.

athletic exercise, but if the science of boxing was more generally practiced throughout the country, and the various contests were governed by a set of rules that strictly and strongly precluded even the possibility of anything like brutality, I think that sparring would soon become as popular and universal as it is useful and beneficial to the development of the best faculties of the body.

PART FOUR
THE RULES

THE RULES

At present there are two recognized codes under which all boxing contests are held, viz.: the London Prize Ring Rules, which regulate all championship fights with bare knuckles, and are only used by professionals. They admit of every license, and are not fit to be considered by amateurs. The rules that govern all amateur meetings, both in this country and in England, are known as the "Marquis of Queensbury's Rules," but even these, although they are free from most of the worst features of their prototype, still leave much to be desired.

On the basis of the Queensbury rules, Mr. David Blanchard, of Boston, Mass., has framed a new code which has not as yet been published, but has been warmly endorsed by many prominent lovers of the manly art. They seem to me to correct the most objectionable features of the Queensbury rules, and if generally adopted, will encourage fairer and more harmless, and at the same time more scientific and interesting exhibitions of the old and much admired sport. I append them to this treatise in the hope that they will receive from the hands of amateurs the favorable reception they deserve, and I trust that the general impression will be that they fully deserve the heading of the "American Fair-Play Rules."

The American Fair-Play Rules

1. An honest and competent referee must be chosen who should be familiar with the rules. His orders must be promptly obeyed, and his decisions in all cases shall be final.
2. A responsible timekeeper must be appointed who shall take his position near the ropes, and should be provided with a proper time-watch. The referee also may have the privilege of keeping time for his own satisfaction, particularly in reference to the

twelve seconds after a fall.

3. All contests should take place in a roped square enclosure, twenty feet square or as near that as possible, with eight posts, which should be padded on the inside. Three ropes of one-inch diameter should be used, the top one to be four feet from the floor or ground and the others at equal distances below it or sixteen inches apart. There should be a circle three feet in diameter drawn in the middle of the enclosure, to be known as the center, where contestants shall meet for the beginning of each round.

4. Each principal may have two attendants, only one of whom shall be allowed within the enclosure. While the contest is in progress the attendants must take positions outside the ring and neither advise nor speak to either of the principals, except while they are resting. A violation of this rule may be punished by the referee excluding the offender from serving as an attendant. Either attendant may quietly call the attention of the referee to any violation of the rules. While resting, principals may use a light chair in their corners, but it must be placed outside by the attendants while the contest is in progress.

5. No wrestling, clinching, hugging, butting, or anything done to injure an opponent except by fair and manly boxing, shall be allowed. If a contestant should resort to clinching, his opponent may continue hitting as long as he does not clinch himself. A contestant shall not go to the floor to avoid his opponent to obtain rest, nor shall he strike his opponent when down or on one or both knees, nor be allowed to strike below the belt or waist. No feeling should exist between contestants, and the custom of shaking hands before and after the contest should never be omitted.

6. A round shall be of three (3) minutes' duration, with one minute between rounds for rest, and the time occupied in verbal contention or discussion shall be noted by the timekeeper, and it shall not be included as part of a round. In all matches the number of rounds and weight of gloves should be mutually agreed upon. It is suggested that the gloves should not weigh over three ounces each.

7. If a glove shall burst or come off it must be replaced immediately to the satisfaction of the referee. No tampering with the gloves

by forcing the hair from the knuckles or otherwise, shall be allowed. The costume shall be tights, with stockings and light shoes and shirt if desired.

8. If either man is sent to the floor, or accidentally falls, he shall be allowed 12 seconds to rise and opponent shall retire to his corner and remain until the fallen man shall first reach the center, when time shall be called and the round completed. If, however, the man fails to come to the center within 12 seconds, the referee shall decide that he has lost the contest.

9. If a man is forced on to the ropes in such a manner as to be in a position where he is unable to defend himself, it shall be the duty of the referee to order both men to the center.

10. If either principal becomes so exhausted that it is apparently imprudent to continue, it shall be the duty of the referee to stop the contest and give his decision in favor of the more deserving man.

11. Spectators should not be allowed within three (3) feet of the enclosure.

12. If at any time during the contest it should become evident that the parties interested or bystanders are doing anything to injure or intimidate either principal or to willfully interfere in any way to prevent him from fairly winning, the referee shall have the power to declare the principal so interfered with the winner. Or if at any time the ring is broken into to prevent the principals from finishing the contest, it shall then also be the duty of the referee to award the contest to the man who at times in his opinion had the advantage.

13. If on the day named for the meeting anything unavoidable should occur to prevent the contest from taking place or from being finished, the referee shall name the time and place for the next meeting, which must be within three days from the day of the postponement, proper notice of which shall be given to both parties. Either man failing to appear at the time and place appointed by the referee shall be deemed to have lost the contest.

14. If there is anything said or done to intimidate the referee while serving, or if the referee has any other good and sufficient reasons why his decision should not be immediately rendered, he shall have the right to reserve his decision, which, however,

must be rendered within 24 hours after the contest.

15. If the contest should occur in a field, blunt hobbles not over one-eighth of an inch in thickness or length shall be used in place of spikes on the soles of the shoes, and must be placed so as to be harmless to an opponent.

16. In order that exhibitions may be conducted in a quite and orderly manner, the referee should always request spectators to refrain from loud expressions or demonstrations, and any one guilty of such conduct while a contest is in progress should be severely condemned.

Suggestion to referee: While in the foregoing rules broad and unrestricted powers are reposed in the referee in order that his authority may be unquestioned in preventing intentional violations of the rules and of fair dealing, it is expected that the referees will use the greatest caution and wisest discretion in the exercise of their power and in distinguishing accidental mistakes on the part of the contestants or their supporters from willful violations of the spirit of these articles.

London Prize Ring Rules

1. That the ring shall be made on turf, and shall be four-and-twenty feet square, formed of eight stakes and ropes, the latter extending in double lines, the uppermost line being four feet from the ground, and the lower two feet from the ground. That in the center of the ring a mark to be formed, to be termed the scratch.

2. That each man shall be attended to the ring by two seconds and a bottle-holder. That the combatants, on shaking hands, shall retire until the seconds of each have tossed for choice of position, which, adjusted, the winner shall choose his corner according to the state of the wind or sun, and conduct his man thereto; the lose taking the opposite diagonal corner.

3. That each man shall be provided with a handkerchief of a color suitable to his own fancy, and that the seconds shall entwine these handkerchiefs at the upper end of one of the center stakes. That these handkerchiefs shall be called "Colors," and that the winner of the battle at its conclusion shall be entitled to their possession as the trophy of victory.

4. The two umpires shall be chosen by the seconds or backers to watch the progress of the battle, and take exception to any breach of the rules hereafter stated. That a referee shall be chosen by the umpires, unless otherwise agreed on, to whom all disputes shall be referred; and that the decision of this referee, whatever it may be, shall be final and strictly binding on all parties, whether as to the matter in dispute or the issue of the battle. That the referee shall be provided with a watch for the purpose of calling time; the call of that referee only to be attended to, and no other person whatever shall interfere in calling time. That the referee shall withhold all opinion till appealed to by the umpires, and that the umpires strictly abide by his decision without dispute.

5. That on the men being stripped, it shall be the duty of the seconds to examine their drawers; and, if any objection arises as to insertion of improper substances therein, they shall appeal to their umpires, who, with the concurrence of the referee, shall direct what alteration shall be made.

6. That the spikes in the fighting boots shall be confined to three in

number, which shall not exceed three-eighths of an inch from the sole of the boot, and shall not be less than one-eighth of an inch broad at the point; two to be placed in the broadest part of the sole, and one in the heel; and that in the event of a man's wearing any other spikes, either in the toes or elsewhere, he shall be compelled either to remove them or provide other boots properly spiked, the penalty for refusal to be loss of the stakes.

7. That both men being ready, each shall be conducted to that side of the scratch next to his corner previously chosen; and the seconds on the one side, and the men on the other, having shaken hands, the former shall immediately leave the ring, and there remain till the round be finished, on no pretence whatever approaching their principals during the round, without permission from the referee. The penalty to be the loss of the battle to the offending parties.

8. That at the conclusion of the round, when one or both of the men shall be down, the seconds shall step into the ring and carry or conduct their principal to his corner, there affording him the necessary assistance, and that no person whatever be permitted to interfere in this duty.

9. That on the expiration of 30 seconds the referee appointed shall cry "Time," upon which each man shall rise from the knee of his second and walk to his own side of the scratch unaided; the seconds immediately leaving the ring. The penalty for either of them remaining eight seconds after the call of time to be the loss of the battle to his principal, and that either man failing to be at the scratch within eight seconds shall be deemed to have lost the battle.

10. That on no consideration whatever shall any person, except the seconds or the referee, be permitted to enter the ring during the battle, nor till it shall have been concluded; and that in the event of such unfair practice, or the ropes or stakes being disturbed or removed, it shall be in the power of the referee to award the victory to that man who, in his honest opinion, shall have the best of the contest.

11. The seconds shall not interfere, advise, or direct the adversary of their principal, and shall refrain from all offensive and irritating expressions, in all respects conducting themselves with order and decorum, and confine themselves to the diligent and careful

discharge of their duties to their principals.

12. That in picking up their men, should the seconds willfully injure the antagonist of their principal, the latter shall be deemed to have forfeited the battle on the decision of the referee.

13. That it shall be a fair "stand-up fight," and if either man shall willfully throw himself down without receiving a blow, *whether blows shall have previously been exchanged or not,* he shall be deemed to have lost the battle; but that this rule shall not apply to a man who in a close slips down from the grasp of his opponent to avoid punishment, or from obvious accident or weakness.

14. That butting with the head shall be deemed foul, and the party resorting to this practice shall be deemed to have lost the battle.

15. That a blow struck when a man is thrown or down shall be deemed foul. That a man with one knee and one hand on the ground, or with both knees on the ground shall be deemed down; and a blow given in either of those positions shall be considered foul, providing always that, when in such position, the man so down shall not himself strike or attempt to strike.

16. That a blow struck below the waistband shall be deemed foul, and that in a close, seizing an antagonist below the waist, by the thigh, or otherwise, shall be deemed foul.

17. That all attempts to inflict injury by gouging, or tearing the flesh with the fingers or nails, and biting, shall be deemed foul.

18. That kicking, or deliberately falling on an antagonist with the knees or otherwise when down, shall be deemed foul.

19. That all bets shall be paid as the battle money, after a fight is awarded.

20. The referee and umpires shall take their positions in front of the center stake, outside the ropes.

21. That due notice shall be given by the stakeholder of the day and place where the battle money is to be given up, and that he be exonerated from all responsibility upon obeying the direction of the referee; that all parties be strictly bound by these rules; and that in future all articles of agreement for a contest be entered into with a strict and willing adherence to the letter and spirit of these rules.

22. That in the event of a magisterial or other interference, or in case of darkness coming on, the referee [or stakeholder in case

no referee has been chose] shall have the power to name the time and place for the next meeting, if possible on the same day, or as soon after as may be. In naming the second or third place, the nearest spot shall be selected to the original place of fighting where there is a chance of its being fought out.

23. That should the fight not be decided on the day all bets shall be drawn, unless the fight shall be resumed the same week, between Sunday and Sunday, in which case the referee's duties shall continue, and the bets shall stand and be decided by the event. The battle money shall remain in the hands of the stakeholder until fairly won or lost by a fight, unless a draw by mutually agreed upon, or, in case of a postponement, one of the principals shall be absent, when the man in the ring shall be awarded the stakes.

24. That any pugilist voluntarily quitting the ring, previous to the deliberate judgment of the referee being obtained, shall be deemed to have lost the fight.

25. That on an objection being made by the seconds or umpire the men shall retire to their corners, and there remain until the decision of the appointed authorities shall be obtained; that if pronounced "foul," the battle shall be at an end; but if "fair," "time" shall be called by the party appointed, and the man absent from the scratch in eight seconds after shall be deemed to have lost the fight. The decision in all cases to be given promptly and irrevocably, for which purpose the umpires and the referee should be invariably close together.

26. That if a man leaves the ring, either to escape punishment or for any other purpose, without the permission of the referee, unless he is involuntarily forced out, shall forfeit the battle.

27. That the use of hard substances, such as stones, or sticks, or resin, in the hand, during the battle, shall be deemed foul, and that on the requisition of the seconds of either man the accused shall open his hands for the examination of the referee.

28. That hugging on the ropes shall be deemed foul. That a man held by the neck against the stakes, or upon or against the ropes, shall be considered down, and all interference with him in that position shall be foul. That if a man in any way makes use of the ropes or stakes to aid him in squeezing his adversary, he shall be deemed the loser of the battle; and that if a man in a

close reaches the ground with his knees, his adversary shall immediately loose him or lose the battle.

29. That all glove or room fights be as nearly as possible in conformity with the foregoing rules.

The Marquis of Queensbury Rules

For the English Challenge Cups (open to Gentlemen Amateurs)
1. That the entries be drawn to contend by lots.
2. That the entrance fee be --.
3. Heavyweights to be over 158 lbs.; middleweights not to exceed 158 lbs.; lightweights not to exceed 140 lbs.
4. That there be three judges appointed by the committee.
5. That the boxing take place in a 24-foot ring.
6. That no wrestling, roughing, or hugging on the ropes be allowed.
7. That each heat consist of three rounds, with one minute interval between each; the duration of each round to be at the discretion of the judges, but not to exceed five minutes.
8. Any competitor not coming up to time shall be deemed to have lost.
9. That no shoes or boots with spikes or sprigs be allowed.
10. Competitors to wear jerseys.
11. Gloves be provided by the club.
12. The cups to be boxed for once in each year; the winner to receive a silver medal.

Contests for Endurance

1. To be a fair and stand-up boxing match, in a 24-foot ring, or as near that size as practicable.
2. No wrestling or hugging allowed. The rounds to be of three minutes' duration, and one minute time.
3. If either man fall, through weakness or otherwise, he must get up unassisted, 10 seconds to be allowed him to do so, the other man meanwhile to retire to his corner, and when the fallen man is on his legs the round is to be resumed and continued until the three minutes have expired, and if one man fails to come to the scratch in the 10 seconds allowed, it shall be in the power of the referee to give his award in favor of the other man.
4. A man hanging on the ropes in a helpless state, with his toes off the ground, shall be considered down. No seconds or any other person to be allowed in the ring during the rounds.
5. Should the contest be stopped by any unavoidable interference, the referee to name time and place for finishing the contest as

soon as possible, so that the match must be won or lost, unless the backers of both men agree to draw their stakes.

6. The gloves to be fair-sized boxing gloves of the best quality, and new.
7. Should a glove burst or come off, it must be replaced to the referee's satisfaction.
8. A man on one knee is considered down, and if struck, is entitled to the stakes.
9. No shoes or boots with spikes allowed.

English Definition of an Amateur

Any gentleman who has never competed in an open competition, or for public money, or for admission money, or with professionals for a prize, public money, or admission money, and who has never at any period of his life taught, pursued, or assisted in the pursuit of athletic exercises as a means of livelihood. The committee reserves the right of requiring a reference or of refusing an entry.

American Definition of an Amateur

An amateur is any person who has never competed in an open competition, or for a stake, or for public money, or for gate money, or under a false name; or with a professional for a prize, or where gate money is charged; nor has ever, at any period of his life, taught or pursued athletic exercises as a means of livelihood.

ADDENDUM

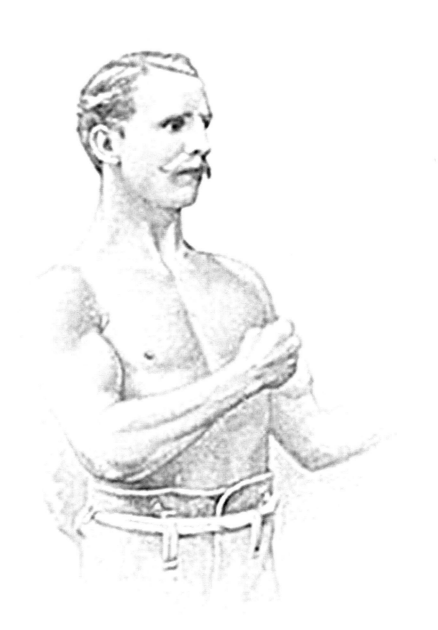

WILLIAM "BILLY" EDWARDS IS DEAD

Once a Champion Pugilist Himself, He Also Trained John L. Sullivan

New York Times
August 13, 1907

William H., better known as "Billy" Edwards, one of the last of the old-time prizefighters, died yesterday morning of Bright's Disease at the home of his brother Joseph Edwards of 99 First Place, Brooklyn. He was 63 years old. Edwards came to this country from England when a young man, and instantly won recognition in the prize ring.

In 1868 he won the title of lightweight champion of the world by defeating Sam Collyer in a bare-fist fight. He defended the title against all comers and retained it until 1884, when he fought Charley Mitchell at Madison Square Garden in one of the first glove bouts ever seen in this country. The fight was stopped by the police, but not until it was clear that Mitchell had all the best of it.

In 1882 Edwards became house detective at the Hoffman House and remained in the place for many years, in which time he was one of the most familiar figures around the hotel and was the favorite stakeholder for the politicians and sporting men who used to make the hotel their headquarters. On several occasions just before an election or big sporting event, Edwards was known to have nearly a million dollars in his possession as a stakeholder.

Edwards left the hotel in 1896 and devoted himself to his boxing pupils. He trained John L. Sullivan for his famous battles with Paddy Ryan and Joe Goss and was always recognized as an authority on ring matters.

His health had been growing constantly worse for some months, and a few week ago he moved to Atlantic City with his family. Mrs. Edwards was there at the time of her husband's death, a baby girl having arrived in the family only a week ago. Edwards had another child, a son, by a former wife. He is a lawyer and is at present traveling in California.

THE STATE OF LOUISIANA VERSUS THE OLYMPIC CLUB

In 1894, the State of Louisiana sued the Olympic Club of New Orleans, the home of numerous fights, including Gentleman Jim Corbett's victory over John L. Sullivan. The state sought to shut down prizefighting in New Orleans. The case (*State v. Olympic Club*, 24 L.R.A. 452, 15 So 190) went through numerous appeals, eventually ending up in the Supreme Court, which upheld the state's position, effectively ending boxing in Louisiana for some time.

During the course of the legal fight, Billy Edwards' *The Art of Boxing and Manual of Training* was used as a reference in court, which gave the book a unique position in history. The following two news reports from the *New York Times* have been included in this volume to provide the reader some historical background on the subject.

OLYMPIC CLUB WINS

Judge Rightor Says the Law to Prohibit Prize Fighting is a Fraud

The New York Times
March 12, 1895

NEW ORLEANS, La. March 11. - Today prize fighting again received encouragement from the New Orleans judiciary. Some months ago the Attorney General filed suit against the Olympic Club, demanding the forfeiture of its charter because prizefights had been held in its arena. The jury rendered a verdict In favor of the club. The State carried the case to the Supreme Court, which sent the matter back to the District Court for a new trial. Judge Rightor today rendered judgment In favor of the club, and his decision will allow prize fighting in the future.

The Judge finds that there is no real distinction between a glove contest and a prizefight, but I that the present law is not adequate to prevent either. "The act prohibiting," says the Judge in his decision, "is a piece of legislative fraud and mendacity; It neither defines the crime of prizefighting nor does it provide any penalty for the crime which cannot be evaded by the mockery of covering with gloves the hands of the gladiators.

"That a glove contest is as brutal and as dangerous as a prizefight was settled In the case of Lavigne vs. Andy Bowen. On the whole, I find that prizefighting in Louisiana is a glove contest, and that a glove contest is a prizefight. It logically follows that there is no prohibition of glove contests in this State, the same being legalized and encouraged under certain conditions which the prizefighter willingly accepts. Prizefighting is now what it never was before the enactment of Statute 25 of 1890, a legitimate business and domestic industry, under the special protection of the law, while before the passage of that statute it would constitute the crime of assault and battery, and in some cases of manslaughter."

NO MORE FIGHTS IN NEW ORLEANS

The New York Times
May 7, 1895

NEW ORLEANS, La. May 6. - The Supreme Court today decided against the Olympic Club, knocking out the fights before that institution. This is the second opinion in the case, the court having on the first hearing remanded the matter. Judge Rightor's decision affirming the right of the club to give prizefights was thus set aside today by the higher tribunal. The result is a deathblow to prizefights in this city.

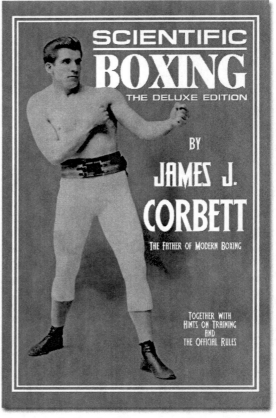

Printed in the United Kingdom
by Lightning Source UK Ltd.
135545UK00001B/108/P